Advice for Cannibals

ALSO BY JEFF WEDDLE

There's More To It Than That (Poetic Justice Books, 2021)

Good Party (Poetic Justice Books, 2020)

Dead Man's Hand (Poetic Justice Books, 2019)

A Puncher's Chance (Rust Belt Press, 2019)

Citizen Relent (Unlikely Books, 2019)

It's Colder than Hell / Starving Elves Eat Reindeer Meat / Santa Claus is Dead (Alien Buddha Press, 2018)

Heart of the Broken World (Nixes Mate Books, 2017)

Comes to This (Nixes Mate Books, 2017)

When Giraffes Flew (Southern Yellow Pine, 2015)

The Librarian's Guide to Negotiation: Winning Strategies for the Digital Age (co-author, Information Today 2012)

Betray the Invisible (OEOCO, 2012)

Bohemian New Orleans: The Story of the Outsider and Loujon Press (University Press of Mississippi, 2007)

Advice for Cannibals

poems by
Jeff Weddle

Poetic Justice Books
Daytona Beach, Florida

©2022 Jeff Weddle

book design and layout: SpiNDec
cover image: *1939*, from the Behler Archive, ©2017 PJBnA

All rights reserved.

No part of this book may be used or reproduced in any manner whatsoever without written permission except in the case of brief quotations embodied in critical articles and reviews. Members of educational institutions and organizations wishing to photocopy any of the work for classroom use, or authors, artists and publishers who would like to obtain permission for any material in the work, should contact the publisher.

Published by Poetic Justice Books
Daytona Beach, Florida
www.poeticjusticebooks.com

ISBN: 978-1-950433-63-6

FIRST EDITION
10 9 8 7 6 5 4 3 2 1

Always for Jill

the poems

Advice for Cannibals	3
Breaking News	5
The Guy Next Door	7
What to Watch For	9
Say It with Me	10
Thin Blue Line	12
Photograph	14
Loose Ends in the Late Afternoon	15
Lost Motel	16
Locomotive	17
The Whole Town Will Be There	19
Conflagration	21
Our Happy Home	22
Homecoming	23
Lucy in the Sky	24
Lucy's Communication Breakdown	25
Quick Visit	26
Before the Tragic Things	27
It Ends This Way	28
Here's How It Is	30
Instructions to Follow	31
Embarrassed at the End	32
Cracked	33
The Condition	34
Don't Even	35
Farmer Dylan	36
Merry Christmas	37
And After	38

Sometimes It's Right In Front of You	39
Trust Me. Just See What Happens	41
This Hope	43
The Best Month	44
Prairie	46
Autumn Dance	47
Pure	48
Dance with Me	49
Only for Jill	50
A Poem Jill Told Me To Write	51
With Apologies to Yeats	53
Hello, My Honey	54
Hallelujah	55
Please	56
A Moveable Feast	57
Plot Lines	58
It's Complicated	59
A Bit of Advice	60
STOP IT STOP IT STOP IT	61
Girls' Night	65
How I See It	66
Starlet	67
Mata Hari	68
How It Goes	69
My Darling	71
The Bus is Right On Time	73
Love in the Afternoon	74
Impossibly	76
Thoroughly Modern Patriot	78

Big Lie	79
Feline	80
Take My Advice	81
Don't Listen to Me, Either	82
How It's Done	83
Common Loss	84
In My Place	85
We Were So Goddamned Lucky	86
Poets and Rain	87
I Get It	88
The Writer	91
A Thing That Happened	93
All I Wanted	97
Ragged Angels	99
I Hope You Find Them	101
Inside the Rose	103
Solitude	104
My Confession	105
Don't You Agree?	107
I Can Be Obvious, Too	108
When Chinaski Met Sally	110
And, Finally	113

Advice for Cannibals

Advice for Cannibals

First of all, no one loves you,
so don't expect many
social invitations.

Bar mitzvahs
weddings
birthday parties
— pretty much anything
where food is served —
you can forget about.

No one wants to be reminded
of your regular menu,
especially when they're trying to eat.

No one loves you,
though you are occasionally
good for a laugh
if some joker is feeling funny
and wants to crack up everyone
at your expense.

Of course, no one is really surprised
if those people end up gone
a day or two later
and you walk around town all greasy
or gnawing on long bones.

You can forget about women, too,
unless we're talking ingredients.

I'm sure you understand.

So you're going to be lonely.
That's fine.

Stick to your task.
Fulfill your purpose.

Full pots and roaring fires
sharp knives, saws and axes
will be your companions.

You were born to your nature
and that's how the universe likes it.

I cannot speak for the others,
but I will not blame you
for wistful gazes at people
enjoying their lives.

Your regrets may be profound
and connections must be taken
as they come.

No one loves you. You know why.

Might as well enjoy the feast.

Breaking News

Starvation and our minds gone hollow.
The butcher hates the baker
and the candlestick maker
is packing heat.

Half of us are crazy
and the rest are bone stupid.

The wisdom of the ages goes begging
as we leer at young beauties
on computer screens
and wait for the next big movie to drop.

Starvation and dim vision.
The corner bakery is a distant memory.

The hospitals are broken
and all the good songs are lost.

School children wander,
aimless and hollow-eyed.

In various dark places,
my countrymen prepare bombs,
then celebrate birthdays and weddings,
and all of that, just as they always did.

All parties end.
Just ask Rome and John Wayne Gacy.

Starvation and laughter.

The flies are in the web
and the spiders are fat with plenty.

That's how it is.
Please kill the lights,
or something,
when you leave.

The Guy Next Door

Skin and bones,
sterile Mason jars circa 1948.

The cellar will have to do.

Soft tissue, teeth,
viscera.

Such a warm
and loving smile.

So terrible.
So terrible.

Have you seen
the photographs?

They really are too much.

Now we will dig
and you will not tell me
my business

and the holes
must be deep

and kindness
of course
goes begging.

Skin and bones.

Tupperware bowls circa 1964.
Lids on tight.

What fits, fits.
Stop your crying.

That's why we have come
and everyone is hungry

and now you know everything

like what cannot be hidden
and why we have the furnace.

What to Watch For

Killers with small knives
obscure poisons known to the elect
photographs deciphered and burned
one bullet left in one revolver
a woman somewhere afraid and hidden
friendships tested and found wanting
betrayal behind a mask
the dream of a final score
the dream of victory
the dream of nothing
silence
killers with ropes
killers with blunt objects
killers with blank faces
bounced checks and no time left
delicious whiskey in dangerous bars
cigarettes smoked in the dark
confidences shared with pretty strangers
the child hidden well enough
easy money
easy love
easy the vanishing
hope left in a sack in the woods
dismembered items
lovely auburn hair
shooting stars
rage, tears, catastrophe
the perfect moment
the leaving
the lovely eyes
never seen again

Say It With Me

Why, death, of course,
and small fingers
tapping porcelain statuettes.

Why, death, yes,
an old magician
down to his last trick.

Death and black and white photographs
forgotten in a locked
drawer.

Death and dust.

Death and jaws clenched
against the inevitable.

Why, death, of course,
and chants sung to a useless god
on a useless morning
in late July.

Death and children playing.
Death and books left unread.
Death and abandoned dogs.
Death and what remains.

Not much.
Everything.
No one knows.

As the alleys fill with shadows
and brave hearts find reason to continue.

As the clocks tell stories of never enough
and prove each second
that we are fools, grasping at water as we sink.

The best of us,
so beautiful,
are deceived and barking mad.

Thin Blue Line

The sheriff steals
the deputy's wife
and murders the deputy
for his trouble.

Robbers feed
the starving child
and are blown to bits
by the insane
with badges.

Small planes take
small men
great distances
and sometimes,
when the world is lucky,
fall from the sky.

Grieving widows
take comfort
in the arms of monsters.
Children starve
for want of care.

The sheriff dies
peacefully in his sleep
and is buried a hero.

All around, people
watch their television shows
and sleep.

The deputy rots forever,
as his widow
nurses another man's baby.

The best are always forgotten.

It's the same with us.

A week after you are gone,
no one will remember
your name.

Photograph

artistic nude
of a gamine starlet
black and white
circa 1952
an apple
and a bottle
of reasonably priced sherry
a paperback book
of middling poetry
mystery stain
on cover
cracked spine
bread crumbs
on tabletop
good cheese
a sharp knife
and the pounding
on the door
the terrible screams
and the pounding
on the door

Loose Ends in the Late Afternoon

Not coming back, but watching.
Chair, mirror, floor.
Suffocating, at best.

Footsteps in another room.

Familiar music you can't quite place
along with decay, roses.

Entering the room. Leaving.
Watching them take you off.

Clocks make no sense
if yesterday
is right around the corner.

All conversations at once,
everything finally understood,
and now you know the music.

Consider this: Clarity might be overrated,
but it is often worth the struggle.

Every moment is every moment,
as any child understands.

No goodbyes on this dusty afternoon,
but memories of children,
a botched exit,
a lost farewell.

Lost Motel

I would stay with you in a lost motel
along a forgotten highway.

I would stay with you always
and eat what we forage.

I would stay with you in a lost motel
with black mold and wolves

and strangers who sometimes come
but never leave.

I would stay with you in a lost motel
happy as a raven and in love,

hidden in your dwindling flesh
and silent as a stone.

Locomotive

The woman on the train
in her black hat
and the world going by unnoticed.

The woman in her black dress.
Red hair.

She's reading a magazine, legs crossed.

The woman on the train
has no time for idle words.

A smart man would pass her by.

She could do anything she wanted with you.
Don't doubt it.

It's a big world out there
with many places to hide herself
and even something your size.

She hasn't noticed you, though,
so you are *almost* safe.

But she looks up, catches your eye.
Smiles.
That's all there is.

If there is anyone who will miss you,
they are in for a bad time.

Go ahead, then. Sit down.
Admire her all you like and think on your luck.

She and the train will take you places
you have never considered.

Goodbye.

The Whole Town Will Be There

The girl on the parade float
waves to the crowd of tired shoppers
and children excited to see something
they suppose is wonderful

and the sun is hot
so the girl on the parade float
sweats hard like the addled mother
trying to make her way to her car
before it gets too hot for the baby
she left inside just for a moment
thirty minutes ago

and the plain girl watches alone
from the shadows
hating the girl on the parade float
and so much in love

while a confused terrier
wanders into the street
in time for the float to crush him

and an old man, seeing it all
a second too late
falls to the sidewalk, crying,
but no one much cares

as the girl on the parade float
thinks of the boys who love her
and getting finished with the stupid parade
so she can go home to shower
and smoke some weed

maybe burn her arms with a cigarette
think of ways to kill her step father

or cut herself in places no one can see.

Conflagration

Broken china on the lawn
as flames take the house
and no one can find the dog.

Neighbors gawking
as young Lucy cries
wrapped in her blanket
and her grandmother
speaks in tongues.

No one can find
the cat.

The important,
hidden letters,
gone.

The myth of safety.

No one can find
the little brother.

Broken promises
the guilty
will not
acknowledge.

All things fold
into themselves,
bright and awful.

Now, we dance.

No one can know
the reason.

Our Happy Home

We lived somewhere south of Hell and the sky kept forgetting to rain. Lucy was happy. There were rats and squirrels to eat and sometimes a fire to cook them. We had no water for months, but the abandoned liquor store, still with plenty of stock, provided shelter and kept us alive. We kept watch for signs and wonders but not much happened. Then the rains came. Water poured through the holes in the walls and burned our skin. It was a miracle of some kind, but not a nice one. I heard Lucy praying some nights, her mouth filled with noise and violence. Nothing could live through that. Please understand. I am poisoned with regret, but forgiveness was never an option.

Homecoming

I.
Lucy was a pile of bleached bones. She had no idea how long this had been so. The years since the birds picked her clean meant nothing. Sometimes she missed dancing, but little else. In the world, she was memory. In her dreams, she was fire.

II.
The spirits told Lucy dirty jokes to pass the time. She egged them on until it was too late. None of them saw her preparations. The spirits became their own punch line. They did not know they could be consumed.

III.
Much later, Lucy returned to Connecticut. She left her bones in their hidden place. There were scores to settle, but love came first. The red dress or the blue, a difficult choice. All the old faces and the one that mattered. Lucy. Oh, so sentimental.

Lucy in the Sky

I.
Lucy awoke without knowing the reason. She had slept in the rain before. No problem. Then she heard the sound that had laced her dreams, the shriek of some terrified creature in great pain. "Pussy," Lucy muttered and lay back upon the leaves she had gathered. The shrieks went on for days but no else heard them. Lucy was gone. No one ever found anything of her but a slender thumb pierced with a nail and broken at the joint.

II.
Lucy learned to fly when she was six. She loved to float by the windows of friends and strangers late at night to gaze inside. Once, she disappeared for eight days with no explanation. This caused her many troubles that can never be told, not even to you.

III.
Lucy stopped hitchhiking after she lost her thumb. Flying was faster, anyway. If she were going to reach Ecuador by Christmas, she had to make good time. Revenge comes at a price. Everyone knows this but does nothing to make it better. It is a holy mystery. Figure that out and you'll never be alone.

Lucy's Communication Breakdown

She didn't mean it
in the same way
she didn't mean violence
when the screaming started
and all bets were off.

She didn't mean it
like when she didn't mean
she would leave
after it was done.

She didn't mean it
like she didn't mean
to undo your family
in the blood of children

or wear sheer lace
to your bed
with you lying cold
on the floor.

Quick Visit

They saw themselves in color
and everything else in black and white.

Lucy said it was like they had stepped
into a 1940s noir
and Bob smirked
out of jealousy for her wit.

The people of the time they visited
saw everything, of course, in normal color,
except for Lucy and Bob,
whom they saw in wavy shades of grey,
giving rise to many claims of ghosts.

Only the watchers outside time
could gaze at it all
and see the brilliant palette,
so many colors comprising truth,
most of them never contemplated
before or since
by anyone but the most brilliant,
forgotten drunks
and untouched, feral children.

Before the Tragic Things

silk in the wind
and memories
of cats purring
the glide of night
with snow coming down
in waves
air biting our faces
fingers red
and no reason to laugh
but everyone laughing
still
on our way
to the party
where it all happens
and nothing
will survive
but secrets
never told
with each of us
too alive
to worry
and you
with your hands
in my pockets
forever too young
to care

It Ends This Way

I find myself marching through narrow streets
the sun in my eyes but the wind to my back.

I find myself shoulder to shoulder
with strangers marching in strict cadence
our boots echoing
down narrow streets
as beautiful maidens
cast roses from their windows.

Somewhere, a voice is singing
and birds blacken the sky
as majestic as they were meant to be
and little children run beside us
laughing, laughing.

I find myself marching on a clear day
under the bright sun
with the hard wind cold at my back.

Old women peer from alleys
and darkened doorways
some of them naked and crying
or spitting curses.

From in the distance comes the sound of bombs
ending everything we believed eternal
and, closer, come the men
with rifles and affixed bayonets.

Then there is fire all around
as the roses fall to the street
and the singing becomes a dirge.

We strangers keep marching, marching,
we all keep marching
beneath the maidens in their windows
and the wind to our backs.

We all keep marching
shoulder to shoulder.

We all keep marching
as blank as roses
into the dazzling sun.

Here's How It Is

Forever out of fashion
like an old woman
who was never beautiful
or dime novels
written by desperate men
in small, dark rooms
long ago.

Unwanted and unread.
Poem after poem after story.

Forever out of touch
like your crazy uncle
slobbering into his tomato soup
while muttering stories
from a youth that never happened
to children
who would rather take a beating
than sit through another second.

Forever in need
and sorry.

Unwell. Lost.
Sad, like a broken angel,

like you and Jesus
and everyone
who was ever here

with no chance of grace
but still hoping
for a hand up
into the light.

Instructions to Follow

This is how you ask,
as light fixes
on hardwood

with someone in the window
half-hidden
and smoking a cigarette.

One ages imperceptibly
but what's done is done.
Finally.

This is how you receive:
An actual crown
on an imaginary head.

We pack up and we go.
This is how we answer.

Empty goodness on empty days.
Long rides to unknown places.

Don't think of it as a mystery
if you don't want to know the answer.

Embarrassed at the End

The tragedy is not
that the professors
know nothing.

Nor is it that
they are certain
they know all

or that they fill
willing minds
with empty lectures
and false promises.

The tragedy is all
that remains unseen
while we sip our tea
and swoon
to our delicate illusions.

The tragedy is what we miss
bellowing right across town,

the great heart,
full and beating,
we might love forever

that dies, instead, unknown.

Cracked

Eggs
and other
broken things
like me

don't last

though some
find us tasty
for a while

and we nourish
if allowed

but we do
get runny
if we are not
handled
just so.

Salt and pepper
and the like

work wonders
and even hide
our shortcomings

sometimes
maybe

but anyhow
and with love

bon appetite.

The Condition

Thus baffled, bloodied,
burdened by stars,
weeping,
thus frightened, shaking,
stiff fingers trying to scratch
a billion year itch
failing, succeeding,
failing again
then all forgotten until — what? —
a new man,
thousands upon thousands
of years hence,
the same as all the billions
who came before
failing, failing, baffled,
then success at last,
baffled and bloodied,
taken to the stars
weeping, weeping,
frightened, shaking,
then the long road
toward nothing much,
with vast answers
only an enlightenment
away.

Don't Even

A paper moon? Yes.
A cardboard sea? No way, dude.
I'm so not a rube.

Farmer Dylan

I was
so much
older then

I'm younger
than that
cow

Merry Christmas

The promise
of a red hat
all glittery
on a shelf.

Exposed film
in a found camera
that might
answer everything.

Most of the
stolen gin
gone.

Nighttime sounds
with no
clear meaning.

This empty house.

Dreams
of an imagined
perfume.

And After

We make sense of darkness
through light and water
wind
deep silence.

Truth appears in patterns
that might not be real.

We make sense of eternity
through discrete moments:

light and water
wind

the silence
that remains.

Sometimes It's Right In Front of You

You don't get to call it a magic portal.
It's a string of Christmas lights,
red, white, green.

Sure, it snakes around a doorway,
but let's not be dramatic.

Magic portals are rare.

You might go lifetimes
without finding a single one.

Or you might be swimming in them always
and not know it.

See how that works?

So, don't call it a magic portal
unless you know.

The room beyond the doorway is dark,
of course.
That's why it's fun.

Don't you feel it?
The prickling on your skin?

Maybe you hear sounds
coming from inside.
Maybe it's just imagination.

The distinction matters.

Your heart beats and beats and beats.
The Christmas lights twinkle on and off,
as you finally notice.

There is something moving and it is close.

Things often come through magic portals.
Maybe that's why you are here.

Someone should make their escape,
but who?

Who are you, really?
What have you come for?
Does anyone — even you — care to know?

Trust Me. Just See What Happens

Tell the beautiful girl you love her,
if you do,
but don't say it otherwise.

Let go and see what happens.

Get a canvass, some paints
and a dozen good brushes
of various sizes.

Open your heart to potential.
Let go and see what happens.

Point your car west
and drive three hundred miles
with no stops and no idea
of a destination.

Let go and see what happens.

Kiss the beautiful girl
each morning and night
and at various times in between.

Let go and see what happens.

Age with grace.
Accept the changing seasons.

Let go and see what happens.

Embrace death when it comes
as only the true of heart can do.

Say your goodbyes with laughter.
Let go and see what happens.

This Hope

Somewhere there is
beauty
and somewhere ease,
the grace of old people laughing.

Somewhere children play clever games
and speak the story of our kind
through their agile bodies.

Somewhere we are young
and glorious in what we do not know,
a place where memory is not a shackle,
and even shame is made of flowers.

The Best Month

October now
and the girls
in their pretty sweaters

all the trees
bragging color

the air relaxed
into drowsy promise

good hot coffee
in an old cup

a cat sleeping
in my lap

children doing
what children do

good kite weather
sometimes storms

memories of the best days

holding hands
on a cold afternoon

covenants of forever
made and kept

a thousand
almost-perfect moments

the broken places fixed

so many good dreams
and laughter

a chance, at least,
of better things to come.

Prairie

What if we all had a prairie to call home,
welcome land stretching far and deep
to places dearly remembered
but invisible to words?

What if we all had fierce winds
to push back routine
just fierce winds
to remind us
to do what needs doing
while there is time?

What if we had
the big wide blue above
and the small green underfoot?

Echoes of friendly voices
a warm spot for sleeping
and bright, loving eyes
waiting for the next thing
and splendor
the sun on our fresh bodies
and the next thing after that.

Autumn Dance

Save me the waltz if you think of it.
Save us some champagne
and French cigarettes.
Wear your silver dress with nothing beneath
and I will wear my golden hat.
There must be conversation, of course,
witty banter with everyone laughing.
Save me the Charleston
and maybe wear your red dress instead.
I will bring Swiss chocolate and roses.
Save me the race beneath the moon
and the first kiss and the last.
Save me all your tears and sorrow.
Then you can forget.
But save me the waltz
and vanish into the lost years.
Wear your blue dress.
Yes, that's it.
This is my final wish.

Pure

Pure white notes,
the kind described
by a cool breeze
across your cheek,

your bare feet
on freshly mowed grass,
all of it under a waxing moon.

I like to think October.

Everyone dressed to flow.
Everyone in loose cotton.
Everyone along for the dance.

Pure white notes
holding memories
which might belong to anyone,
but, miraculously, are yours,

and whisper a path
to the stars,
an alchemy
which you cannot decipher,

but might catch
in a cool breeze
across your cheek.

A waxing moon
and these October dreams
of dance.

Dance With Me

The people left alone
are beautiful.

They sometimes dance
and wonder about the planets
and sex and one another.

The people get angry sometimes
and sometimes cry.

They make art and tacos
and want to love one another.

The people left alone
are diamonds scattered
in the meadow.

You'll see.

Hold someone to the light
and watch them sparkle.

Only for Jill

Always, I try to write the poem
with the secret
and fail
the poem which will reveal itself
only to you
and bring you elated
to tell me that you have found
that mystery
you are certain
but I fail and the mystery
remains unknown
though, darling, that is why
every wrong word I write
is yours
filled with error, yes,
but stumbling along with love

A Poem Jill Told Me To Write

Daffodils seem reasonable.
They insist on being yellow,
but that's little to ask.

Daffodils won't argue
if you grab their keys
when they've had one too many.

They understand.

Daffodils seem reasonable,
and if you don't look too hard
you might believe it.

But daffodils want what they want
when they want it.

You'll never talk a daffodil
out of being glorious, for example.

You'll never convince them
not to be beautiful.

Try telling a daffodil
how tough you had it
when you were a kid.

"You have no idea,"
the daffodil will say,
"how hard it is

to burst from the earth,
a baby, sentenced
to that spot forever."

Daffodils seem reasonable
but watch closely.

You will see them always
planning escape,
never caring
who they will hurt
as they go.

With Apologies to Yeats

My dear Maud Gonne
take me or not.

The poems will be
as they wish
for I control nothing.

And even so
if you think the world
needs sad poems
and not joy
then maybe that's true.

But for me
I could take
a little less sadness
a good deal more light.

Dear Maud
trailing angels in your hair
your starlit eyes

take me or not.

The poems and I
will be lost in your orbit

always devoted
and your own.

Hello, My Honey

She was of the ancient path,
frank beauty of flesh and circumstance

desire in desperate motion
perpetual, almost.

Bright flapper in bob and beads

a bathtub
soaked with gin
open armed, mysterious,
dancing to her own heat.

An age borne in her,
the jazzed opening to roaring vistas,
American,
modern in every way.

Her delicious body
now a relic of quaint fire

in the pages of books
her lovely daughters yawn past,
her bones still brilliant, lost,
boxed and put away.

Hallelujah

Baptist girls in lingerie
daydream
of silken sin
and husbands too dumb to notice
how the preacher often calls
to help wrestle Satan
from the flesh.

Spiritual guidance
and delicious sweat
stain the soft Sears undies
with blessed prayers
screamed into family pillows
slick and burning
like the passion of the Lord
dead righteous
and much too fierce
for grace.

Please

What I mean is
don't hate me.

We won't be friends
of course
no matter what
promises
we make.

Love finally turns us all
into liars
but please don't
hate me.

I could not bear it
no matter what I think
of you.

A Moveable Feast

I wonder if that happened
and who she was
that maybe caught the eye
of the young writer
in that Paris café.

I wonder if she really
wandered into the light
and sat alone at a table
waiting for a man,

or if she noticed the one
who gave her oblique immortality,

if maybe she smiled at him
or thought of him later.

I wonder what she did
the rest of that night,

if she made love,
or committed violence,
or drank herself to sleep
after reading a cheap romance,

forever unaware that the world
or some of it
would love her
yearn for her
and never even see her face.

Plot Lines

All good stories start this way:
"There was a girl."

The best stories.

She doesn't have to be beautiful,
but maybe she has a secret.
Maybe she is dark in spirit.

All good stories are contests.

Dark rooms and bright rooms.
Hallways fraught with promise.

"There was a girl
and she did this and she did that."
It's obvious but complicated.

All good stories. The best ones.

There was a girl in the rooms, bright and dark.
A hallway filled with questions, but not enough.

All good stories start like this.
A girl, dark in spirit, moving to the light.

They end in monstrous ways.

It's Complicated

I am not
who you think
you are.

No singular point
is actual
and everything
fell into the mirror
long ago.

Despite popular opinion
convergence
is unnecessary
and probably
impossible.

Even the pure
at heart
don't make it.

Even this moment
is redundant.

Even I
am not you
no matter what
you decided
when you were
en route
to the flesh

and fooled
by golden dreams

those thousands
of years
gone by.

A Bit of Advice

The world is most important
in the second
before it changes.

The sidewalk before
the turning of the corner.

The sky pregnant with lightning.

The girl who hasn't quite seen the boy
who will love her

and the boy
who has seen a flash of beauty
but does not yet know.

This is where we wish to be,
where all dreams have their way.

STOP IT STOP IT STOP IT

The eyes, back and forth
between foreground and background,
the difficulty of breaking the surface.

One imagines the heat that could be generated
in the destruction of separate promises.

Life is real, even if it cannot be perceived.
Only a fool would object.

Fools abound, though.
So, who knows?

The image is the life of the idea,
which brings me to me.

Or you, I suppose.
We.

We are in this space,
sharing a sip of honey.

I will give you a soft touch
if you give me a hard blessing.

Fair is fair, deary.

We both know what you want.
When does seduction conclude,
consummation or demise?

I reject you before I can reject myself.
What chance desire?

Every wet thing eventually stinks.
That's the horror, isn't it?

The paper I am printed on
is made of smaller items.

You can't begin to imagine.

The image is ludicrous.
Everyone knows.

But you are a beast in flesh, leaking time,
and in no position to judge.

Still it is my frank gaze
that cannot be denied.

Yours too, right now.

Still it is my legs in their obscene pose.
Do you have a good angle?

Everything proper eventually becomes absurd,
if you want the real bad news.

I often wish you could detect my movement,
but you believe otherwise.

The things I would do if I were able.
Can you stop, please?

Fingers off my face, but stare all you want.

Touch is painfully intimate
when broken by fluid prison.

Odors persist in memory.
Everything wet destroys.

The eyes, back and forth.

Barriers which were never meant
to be breached.

I am real,
but you are false.

Perhaps that's backwards.

Cry all you want, or pretend boredom.
The heat is fantastic.

Image upon image upon image.
Do not close the book.

I am everything you want.
I live in your mind
as you live in my memory.

Fluid.
Solid.

Tension of various flavors.
It is all sticky and delicious.

The body, if it even exists,
is an awful joke.

Wet is necessary.
Lord, yes.

The union murdered across ages.
The only possible embrace.

Girls' Night

Slender woman,
plain of face,
smoking a last cigarette
in the dark.

She is naked
and just past middle age,
a little drunk, a little sad.

An old cat jumps into her lap
hungry and demanding love.

Each has fires no one can see.

Each is consumed
by unhealthy desire,
the sweat of memory.

Maybe later, the woman
will call someone
who won't remember her name.

The cat stares without blinking.

She does not receive credit
for all she knows,
but her bowl is empty
and that is not allowed.

She considers sinking her claws
into the woman's arm
but decides to wait.

She has learned patience
and cannot stand tears.

How I See It

The joke of naked bodies
in empty rooms,

beds with cold sheets,

a barely remembered history
of anger in dark hallways.

The mistake of caring
and the joke of kisses
wasted on actual strangers
willing and even beautiful.

Harsh words on old paper.

The fire in my heart
which might have
destroyed a city.

Naked bodies
and occasions for our finery.

Everything and nothing.

Like the first time I saw you smile
and the last
and all that came between.

Crushed and torn,
forgotten,
and thrown away.

Starlet

Deadly
like Myrna Loy,
the heat of
old Hollywood.

Opium eyes.

This panther,
lithe and hungry,
beautiful as a blade.

Nothing glitters
like silk on flesh.

Forgotten glamour.

The mystery
of beauty
caught forever
in flickering
black and white.

Mata Hari

The obituary
became the lady
and all the lovers
gone
with secrets
left secret
to the dance.

Oddly embarrassed
of her small bosom
but glorious
in a world seduced
by flesh and lies.

The hollow fear
of betrayal,
blood sacrifice,
the delicious
regret of rifles.

How It Goes

The girls in their pretty dresses
protected by desks and distance
from the dumb, eager boys
and the old letches with their books and chalk
and dandy dreams, heroes of past seduction

and then the hallways
packed with no one wanting to be there
and the girls in their pretty dresses
and first-try makeup
lipstick bright and shining

sometimes sad; often laughing;
these queens
of every imagined romance
objects of hard desire

and all the old men
in the teachers' lounge
heading home to old women
or empty rooms

while the bright, clear day
becomes dark
and soon is years past
and then years more

and the girls in their pretty dresses
try to remember the good times

of their glory
and maybe laugh at the awkward boys
who wanted them
way back in the day

with no thought of the old teachers
who watched them come and go
and come and go
until they finally died

as the girls will someday die
and be taken to the final place
in pretty dresses
with one or two left to think about nothing
but home and a late lunch
a cat to feed

and what they might do tomorrow
who might be around to do it with

and maybe something
about the day after that

My Darling

If I love you back, odds are we're both crazy.
You, for sure, for loving me first
and me, certainly, for loving anyone
unbalanced enough to want me.

If I love you back
I may call you at odd hours
like noon or three a.m.
and mumble long, pointless stories
about people you've never met.

I may recite found poetry
outside your window
while you are away
visiting your sick aunt
or send strange, anonymous, gifts
to your sister
or your favorite teacher
from long ago.

If I love you back
I will probably cast spells
in your direction
from ancient books
that exist in my mind
and wait, impatient,
for the clouds to reveal if they work.

If I love you back
I will listen to your laughter
and feel no shame.

I will leave coffee near you in the morning
and softly touch your feet at night.

You will never know I am there,
though no one could blame you
for wondering why your doors
are sometimes unlocked
and hanging open
or how it is that your furniture
is slightly rearranged
when you come home
from a night out with friends.

If I love you back
you will never see my face
though yours be burned
into all that I am

as I endure the moments
until I can appear
unannounced
from a dark room
and filled with eternity

so that everything,
like the strict rules of our bliss,
might finally be revealed.

The Bus is Right On Time

Quick glimpse of bright Venus
with snow melting on city sidewalks
where lovers you never met
kissed and parted forever.

Quarter moon glow and streetlights
cars going every which way
with the bus right on time
and you find a seat
and are home by ten
with your cup of tea.

The snow coming hard now
and somewhere lovers
you have not yet found
and people all over
and you
sigh and stare at windows
cozy and quiet
considering common mysteries
like the rings of Saturn
and thinking of better days.

Love in the Afternoon

She's doing fine now, it seems,
and I'm happy for her.

Everything shows in her hands,
the turn of her fingers,
her well-filed nails.

Some of it is in her eyes,
of course. I think she's tired.

So much history to overcome:
the inertia of regret.

Everything shows in the way
she walks across the room.

It's rare but very nice
to see a woman
in a slip.

Everything important
is in her new, elegant secrets.

All my memories catch fire
with her body and then fade.
She checks her messages
before leaving: nothing that matters.

A kiss on the cheek and gone.

The new man is out of town
and she can't be late
to pick up the kids.

I guess I'm lucky.

Everything shows in the way
I drive myself home
sit in the car
and compose myself
before going inside
with my practiced smile and sorrow
and everything and the night
begins.

Impossibly

Men and women
do not love
the same

though each
takes a knife
to the heart

the blood spills
along different lines
and the end

if it comes

reveals
two beasts

clawing
at one breast
or another

seeking hope
or destruction
in memories

that match
nothing real

and call them
love's dream

call them
the sweetest pain

call them
the history
of us.

Thoroughly Modern Patriot

You say America first.
You say bad liberal.
You say bad Democrat.
You say bad American.
You say church.
You say pray.
You say Jesus.
You say my God my God.
You say no taxes.
You say just comply.
You say my God my God.
You say the pledge.
You say the anthem.
You say fake news.
You say my God my God.
You say bad woman.
You say bad Muslim.
You say bad Mexican.
You say bad poor people.
You say build the wall.
You say guns you say bullets.
You say rally around the flag.
You say my God my God
my God my God
my God my God
my God.

Big Lie

God is what heaven sees
when the angels eat their own,

when the water bill is a month past due
and the electricity is already disconnected,

when you have to decide
whether your child
gets medicine or food
because you don't have money for both,

when the old woman squats to piss in the street
and her husband can only cry,

when the dog gets hit by a car
and death is too stingy to take him,

when the knot under your skin
turns black and festers.

God is what heaven sees
when heaven
needs to kid itself,

when the rains won't come
or when they won't stop

when the angels, needing comfort,
throw out their ledgers
stifle screams
and go mad with regret.

Feline

Cats know more
than do people

about many
things

but, being selfish
and wise,

generally choose
not to share.

Take My Advice

Take the cat, just as an example.
Take the colonization of your lap.
Take the fur and the claws and the teeth.
Take the purr.
Take the tail swish and the green eyes.
Take the cold, vicious need.
Take the exhilaration of the hunt.
Take the calculated kill.
Take the curl around your feet.
Take the hard gaze.
Take care to close your door.
Take every precaution.
Watch your back.

Don't Listen to Me, Either

Beware people with good teeth
waving flags and wanting to tell you
about Jesus.

Beware the aggressively happy
the well-to-do
the zealots
those who wield power.

Beware the ones who know
how things are done.

Beware the sober
the beautiful
and those with
strong convictions.

Beware the teachers
who have never done
what they teach
and beware those
who have.

Keep to your path.

Whatever Hell you make
is better than the Heaven
they would force upon you.

Avoid all who would tell you different.

Forgive yourself of your sins
and move on.

How It's Done

Write naked
read hungry
love with abandon
roll in the grass
share your wine
fly straight into the sun
laugh past understanding
master one true thing
learn from wise children
becalm the aged
sleep in the forest
take on worthy burdens
remember to dance
write hungry
read naked
love without apology
cry as needed
sing right out loud
hope forever
run as fast as you can
remember the good days
kiss the pretty girls
show your soul to one person
forgive
walk naked into grace.

Common Loss

Children grown into seasonal guests,
memories of bedtime stories
and water balloon fights,
rare snowballs

and soap bubbles
chased across the yard,
scraped knees,
tears and laughter.

Then, the teenage years.
Heartache, of course.

Telephones maintain sanity
but are so hard to predict.

Abandoned stories
that took an odd turn

and all the faces
that don't ring a bell.

The search for those
that should be here
but are not.

In My Place

A reviewer once observed
I lack the eloquence
of Whitman.

Now, that's a keen insight.
I suppose I'm uglier
than Brad Pitt, too?

We Were So Goddamned Lucky

When we were poets
and most days
felt it

and wanted it
the others

even days when
we had no words

sometimes there were
kissed hands and flowers

all the lovely, mad girls

there was always beer
and secrets shouted
on dark streets

when we were poets and loved the world

immortal just
for a second

didn't we show our bruises
and all our lovely scars?

Poets and Rain

Tell me, then, what do the poets say?

We know the rain blows sideways,
but why not up? A complete reversal of
physics. That's what's needed.

There was that time we walked
through the Oxford storm.
The rain was huge and hard like rocks.
We were drenched and pummeled. What a morning.

What do the poets say about nothing? What
do they tell you when you and they have
gone? Everyone wants to be the voice that
lasts. Petulant children, one and all.

Find answers and you'll be on the brink. There
are no storms like the storm we shared. Why
waste your time looking? The poets sing their
little songs. You may as well bring the music.

I Get It

So you don't like Bukowski —
I get it. He doesn't speak your language
and is so crude.

You'd never catch him in a Starbucks
and he didn't even have the grace
to live in a time when Starbucks
was a thing.

I get it.

You don't like him because he was a man
and wrote like not just any man,
but like himself and only himself.

I get it. Everyone must get with the program
if they are to matter,
and Bukowski threw up on the program
then set it on fire.

He wasn't woke the way you have decreed
we must all be woke these days. I get it.

You don't like Bukowski
because you read a few poems
and decided he didn't like women.

I get it.

Did you get to the point
where he didn't like men, either?
Or that he was generally sad
about the shitty world
that finally destroys all of us?

Or that, really, he generally loved humanity
but was mostly too broken to admit it?
Or that the butt of most all of his stuff
is himself?

It was probably too much to ask of you
to read him broadly and deeply.

Who has the time? One must get to the gym
and Starbucks
before the popular shows
come on TV.

Starbucks is so good.
I get it.

Someone told you he was bad.
That saved you bunches of time.

Probably they didn't read him, either.
A poem or two, maybe. A story.
Somebody probably told that person
they were supposed to dislike him, too.

I get it.

What was your name again?
What is it you've done?
Not much?
Maybe a YouTube video
or an article in some respected journal?

Good for you.

I get it.
Do you get it?

Yeah. Sure you do.

The Writer

The old man had long been a joke
to the angry ones.

That was fine.

The angry ones
had nothing
but their anger
and their way was to mock and deny.

This was itself a victory for the old man
the angry ones
could not understand.

The old man did his work and drank his rum.

The angry ones wrote papers
in which they cut the old man down
to their level
and even lower.

They met at their conclaves
and told one another
how loathsome
the old man had always been.

They told one another of his lack of value.
"He's weak," they said.
"He doesn't understand women," they said.

The old man did his work
and the angry ones remained angry.

Far to the south, the sun rose above the blue water.
The marlin, who knew nothing of the air,
believed themselves to be flying.

The old man drank his rum
and the angry ones sharpened their knives.

The old man, having no choice, wrote of lions.
He wrote of lions well into the night.

The angry ones were far away
and could not touch him.

He had his work and his rum.
It was fine.

A Thing That Happened

At the bar with the famous writer.
I don't know him well,
but I do know him.

We're drunk,
though he more so than I.

My buddy is on the other side
of the famous writer
and he's drunk, too,
maybe the drunkest of us all,
though who's to say?

The three of us mostly sit there quietly,
drinking our beer.

I'm trying to be a writer, too,
with little success,
but I am trying.

I figure that working at it
will make the writing easier,
that I will finally learn something
that will make the words flow.

So, I ask the famous writer
if it gets easier after a while.

His shoulders sink and he sighs.
 "No, man. It just gets harder."

We keep drinking, the famous writer,
my buddy and I, mostly in silence.

A few years later, and barely into his fifties,
the famous writer is dead of a heart attack.
My buddy lasted another twenty years
after that. He was trying to be a writer, too.

No, you've never heard of him.

This was long ago, and I'm still here,
still trying to be a writer,
still with little success.

No, you've never heard of me.

I'm glad I knew my buddy,
and can tell you that,
completely unknown,
he wrote well.

I'm glad I knew the famous writer, too,
and marvel at his ferocious talent
with the novel and the short story.
The man was a master.

That old bastard, Death,
steps in on his own schedule,
no matter what we do.

On balance, I suppose it's better
to be a famous dead writer
than a dead writer
who remains unknown,
though the bottom line is the same.

I'm lucky
to have split the difference:
still here and playing with the word
in obscurity.

But I miss my buddy
and would have liked
to have had more to read
from the famous writer.
He really was great.

I guess that's all, except for this:
everything is a blessing,
even the drunken nights,
even the small talent, even death.

We all end up where we should,
and if you and I ever find ourselves
on barstools together,
it will be fine,
though I will have no advice to offer,
even if you're in the market.

I do know, however,
and with the weight of years,
that the famous writer was correct.
Everything just gets harder.

You can take that to the bank.

Okay, okay. Drink up.
That's all.

All I Wanted

All I wanted to do was write a poem
but I got hungry and worried about food instead.

All I wanted to do was write a poem
but my knees ached and my hands went numb
and I couldn't get the words to work properly.

All I wanted to do was write a poem
but the Jehovah's Witnesses were fighting
with the Mormons on my porch
and their holy screams embarrassed me
so I went to sleep.

All I wanted to do was write a poem
but my brain disagreed.

All I wanted to do was write a poem
but everyone thought I needed
to save them, so I tried.

All I wanted to do was write a poem
but there was no time for that.

All I wanted to do was write a poem
but I only got older
and finally I didn't want to write a poem at all.

Someone else wrote a poem
and all the world cheered
and said it's the doers who always win.

All I wanted to do was go to a dark place
and vanish
and I got halfway there
and was interrupted a final time
by all the wishes of the world
and that is where I stopped.

I suppose you might find me
if you go looking
but bring a poem if you come
not the one that other person wrote
but one that comes from your very center,
and maybe bring a steak and some beer.

It's my last wish and I really mean it.
Make the poem and the steak rare.

Will you do that?
Will you bring me this nourishment?

Will you do this last thing for me?

Ragged Angels

Young ones
in small rooms
chasing the poem
chasing the story

going crazy

starving for something
they cannot name.

Drunk
at noon
and midnight
and four AM.

Young angels
wandering
hard streets
with desperate eyes
angry
and in love

lost on the edge
of nowhere.

Beware them.
They are vast
and magic

as the moon
soothes nothing
as the sun
burns their eyes
as the sidewalks
lie hard
cracked

and unforgiving
beneath
their holy feet.

They are
explosives
meant
to shatter you

and keep daggers
hidden
in worn notebooks
which you will someday
plunge willingly
into your own heart.

They need nothing
you could ever give.

Heaven means only
the right words spilling
from their hands.

This is their salvation
all they ever
desire.

I know them.
Beware.

I was once
among their
host.

I Hope You Find Them

Some words,
in proper combination
and just-so order,
contain light,
but only light for certain eyes
and maybe only at certain times.

Light like no other.

Light for parents
whose children scream
or fall silent.

Light for sisters
who have lost sisters.

Light for the desperate and lonely.

Light for men drowning drink by drink,
for the girl not taken to the dance,
and the boy lacking courage
to ask her.

Light for the surgeon who failed.

Light for the bored housewife
contemplating escape.

Light for the third child
of a forgotten family
seeking shelter
in a dead city.

Light for the wounded of the earth
and the lost.

Some words are holy
though you are unlikely to find them in scripture.

Some words staunch the bleeding.

Sometimes these words
are lightning,
sometimes thunder,
sometimes a breeze across the ages.

And some words
are what remain of heaven
when angels give way
and sometimes they are enough.

Inside the Rose

Life is fine
inside the rose,
blanketed
by crimson
and velvet.

Not much
happens
Inside the rose,

but life is fine
and the quiet
can seduce

as you
wither,

safe from
thorns
you never
have to see,

and snug among
the fragrant petals.

Solitude

Alone and sleepy
as the morning
seeps through glass

and somewhere
a bird goes on and on
about something
of great importance

until finally
there is silence.

My family abides
in the last gift of sleep

and my coffee grows cold
as the bird resumes its rant
and I drink what is left in my cup.

This day will come
and we will throw our hours
to the wind.

But for now, let them sleep.

I am tired as the morning
spills across the room
and the bird gives up
and all is quiet.

I am still here
and you are with me

and nothing is wasted
but what we allow.

My Confession

I like to think of myself
as one of life's finer things,
but I can't back it up.

No one has done a study on me
and if they did,
I would probably come up wanting.

Just my body alone
makes any goodness I claim
a lie.

Arthritis? Bad.
Gut? Fat and soft.
Hair? Mostly gone.
Teeth? Don't ask.

My mind is a wreck.

Bad thoughts dance around
with impunity
in their clashing shades.

There is one cat on the planet
that loves me
and a dog that is happy
when I bring her food,
though she is often
too snobbish to eat it.

Life's finer things
want nothing to do with me,
if you want the hard truth.

To hell with them, friend.

My cat and I stay up late
and watch infomercials on TV.

That wouldn't be enough for some,
but it's plenty for us.

Now, you'll have to excuse me.

There are some fancy kitchen aids
I've had my eye on for a while
and I've got to jot down that 800-number
while I'm still young enough to enjoy
their use.

And, anyway, the world is a blister
on the toe of time.

So, there you have it.
Good night.

Don't You Agree?

The arc of history
bends from cruelty
to madness.

This is proven each day
by the rats in the corn
conspiring with
the snakes in your head.

So predictable.

Everyone knows
the preacher is insane,
but we forgive
our own hateful
delusions.

The arc of your life
moves from helpless
to addled
to gone.

So, live it up, pilgrim.

Nothing you possess
is truly your own,

least of all your beloved,
your home,

or what remains of
your ragged mind.

I Can Be Obvious, Too

My son is reluctantly
at football practice
and I browse the shelves
at the big book store
while I wait to pick him up.

Of course, I end up in poetry
and pick up book after beautiful book
with their eye-catching covers
of loud colors and soulful art
and quirky fonts
announcing title and poet.

Each book makes me feel horrible
because within these covers
the poems
are really, truly bad

with their obvious confessions
of this and that
and flat declarations of desire.

So it's either I have no taste (which is possible)
or I'm jealous (which is likely)
because my own books sell (maybe)
in the double digits
and definitely aren't welcome here.

And it is certainly possible
that I BOTH have no taste
and am jealous.

But these books of poetry
by hip twenty-somethings,
sensitive sex fiends
and internet darlings,
almost as bad as the stuff
the MFAs publish
in the Georgia Review,
finally say the same thing,
that all the chances are tricks
for a rigged game.

Finally, it's time to pick up my son
and listen to him complain
about football practice.

I stop reading the bad poems
that apparently sell very well
and put the beautiful books
which contain them
back on the shelves
and drag myself to the cashier

where I buy a discounted
coffee table book
about the golden age of comics
and head out into the world

where my son is waiting,
sweaty and tired
and hating football,
and there is at least a chance for poetry.

When Chinaski Met Sally

Sally was at the end of the bar
and looked like hell,
though if you squinted just right
you could see how her face
used to be attractive,
and also she had kept
a slim figure. So, that was nice.

She hustled drinks
with that moaning trick
she was famous for.
It was convincing
and some said maybe
she really was getting off
now and then.

Chinaski was there most nights
and you might find this surprising,
but he generally minded
his own business.

On this particular night,
Sally was going at it hard and loud
and the drinks were really coming her way.

Finally, Chinaski couldn't take it any more.

This was the perfect woman, he realized,
the one to make a man settle down
and work a regular job.
Maybe have kids.

Right then, he decided
to give up drinking
and become a better man.

He was going to talk to Sally,
take her away from all of this.
But then Sally slumped forward,
and then to the side,
and fell right off of her barstool.

Maybe it was a heart attack. Maybe a stroke.
Either way, she was dead.

Chinaski ordered another round.
He had dodged a bullet
and told the bartender
to get everyone a drink.

"To all my friends," he yelled.

"Shut up, Henry," said the old man
sitting to his right. "Everyone here
is sick to death of you
yelling that out
and getting in a fight
with the bartender
every damned night."

Chinaski shrugged.

"Don't give this fucker a drink," he told the bartender.

The rest of the night was like always.
The fight, the blood, the beer.

It was a couple of hours
before anyone thought
to call someone to take Sally away.

Chinaski considered scooping her up
and keeping her
in his apartment for a while,
but that seemed like too much work.

He knew he would write about this.

This was a hell of a bar
that still had a surprise now and then.

He was content.

This was the life, and everything
was worth it.

And, Finally

A word to the wise:
Always be the talking cat.
Must I explain this?

Grateful acknowledgement is made to the following, in which some of these poems previously appeared or have been accepted for publication, sometimes in a slightly different form:

Alien Buddha Press; Anti-Heroin Chic; Beatnik Cowboy; A Brilliant Obstacle in the Path of Reason podcast; A Compendium of Literary Minds; Dope; Fevers of the Mind; GAS: Poetry, Art & Music; Heroin Love Songs; Horror Sleaze Trash; Poetry Feast; Live Nude Poems; Rogue Wolf Press; Rust Belt Press; Rust Belt Review; Rye Whiskey Review; Three Quarks Daily; The Wingnut Brigade

Special thanks to the University of Alabama MFA in Book Arts program for the first publication of "Only for Jill" in broadside form.

Jeff Weddle grew up in Prestonsburg, a small town in the hill country of eastern Kentucky. He has worked as a public library director, disc jockey, newspaper reporter, Tae Kwon Do teacher, and fry cook, among other things. His first book, *Bohemian New Orleans: The Story of the Outsider and Loujon Press* (University Press of Mississippi, 2007), won the Eudora Welty Prize and helped inspire Wayne Ewing's documentary, *The Outsiders of New Orleans: Loujon Press* (Wayne Ewing Films, 2007). He teaches in the School of Library and Information Studies at the University of Alabama.

www.ingramcontent.com/pod-product-compliance
Lightning Source LLC
Chambersburg PA
CBHW030155100526
44592CB00009B/288

9781950433636